The History

The first major international exhibition of theatre design took place in 1922 at the Municipal Museum (Het Stedelijk Museum) in Amsterdam, presenting the first opportunity for artists of the theatre to congregate since the outbreak of the First World War (fig.1). Exhibitors were challenged 'to give a view of the modern theatre as it is in their imagination', and it had an immediate and profound impact on staging practice in Europe and America.

The exhibition included work by 95 designers and architects from a dozen countries, including Adolphe Appia (1862–1928), Leon Bakst (1866–1924) and Edward Gordon Craig. Cecil Harcourt-Smith, at the time Director of the V&A, recognized the significance of the exhibition, and worked to bring it to London arguing that 'the Museum is the officially constituted centre and home for all branches of Industrial Art and Design, and there is, obviously, no branch of Art covering quite so wide a field as the Theatre which touches Architecture, Painting, Design and Decoration in many forms.'

The exhibition, entitled *International Theatre Exhibition: Designs and Models for the Modern Stage*, came to the V&A in 1923. One of the key exhibits was Edward Gordon Craig's set model for *Hamlet* staged at the Moscow Art Theatre. Directed by Constantin Stanislavsky in 1912 this revolutionary and visionary production changed the direction of theatre design – bringing abstract settings to life. The model was acquired by the V&A after the exhibition in Amsterdam and paved the way for theatre as a subject in a museum. Reconstructed for the 1923 exhibition, the model is made from plaster (fig.2). It epitomises a challenge familiar to the display of performance design – exhibiting objects that survive from a subject whose very essence is ephemeral. Craig's design evolved from his experimentation with moveable screens to create a setting that was not static. The screens, patented by Craig, had four, six, eight, ten or twelve leaves that could fold forward or backward and be moved on the stage by the actors to create different environments and spatial configurations. Difficult to represent in a fixed model, the V&A used the archive, designs and photos of the original model to create an interactive installation of Craig's *Hamlet*, which enables the visitor to manipulate a virtual model of the original production (fig.3).

The International Theatre Exhibition was also the catalyst for establishing a theatre collection at the V&A. Playwright and collector Gabrielle Enthoven had been lobbying the British government to create a theatre museum since 1911. Harcourt-Smith's speech about theatre's central relevance to design made the museum the natural home for her collection, which was accepted in 1924. Her donation was the first of many, including important gifts from the British Council and Arts Council in the 1970s. They provide a comprehensive picture of stage design over the twentieth century.

The Prague Quadrennial and 2011

Founded in 1967 and held every four years, the *Prague Quadrennial of Performance Design and Space* (or PQ) presents work from more than 70 countries on five continents – the spirit of the 1922 International Theatre Exhibition lives on (fig.4). As the world's largest performance design event, PQ covers contemporary work in a variety of disciplines and genres, including design for costume, stage, lighting and sound – as well as theatre architecture for dance, opera, drama, site-specific pieces, multi-media performances and performance art.

The Quadrennial is a festival of performance ideas, creative exchanges, theatrical experiments and a platform to examine the multitude of ways to exhibit scenography (performance design) in its broadest sense. For a moment, the world comes together to live, eat and breathe theatre design, and individual countries compete for attention on a world stage.

The stated purpose of the twelfth Quadrennial, held in 2011, was to examine theatre design in the context of contemporary trends, as well as its links to innovations in other cultural fields – particularly the visual arts, architecture, fashion, installation, video art and new media (fig.5).

The UK is represented by designers selected from an open exhibition organized by the Society of British Theatre Designers (SBTD, fig.6). The society was founded in 1975 by John Bury, Ralph Koltai, Nicholas Georgiadis and Timothy O'Brien, and its mission is to enhance the standing of British theatre design at home and abroad.

This exhibition at the V&A shows the work selected to represent the United Kingdom at the Prague Quadrennial, along with that of a further 25 designers from the UK open exhibition. Peter Farley, Curator for the SBTD, states that 'the aim was to bring the designer for performance out from behind the scenes and reveal his or her vision as an essential collaborator and contributor in the creation of a work of theatre ... nothing exhibited is the final product, the live performance – but a means to communicate the visual possibilities ... models and drawings, beautiful in their own right are displayed as a means of communication.'

4.
Brazil National Exhibition, Prague Quadrennial 2011 (awarded the Golden Triga). Photograph by Martina Novozámská

The Poetics and Technics of Performance Design

There are many interchanges and relationships between theatre and the wider world of art and design. Not only are the language and concerns of contemporary society and culture increasingly loaded with theatrical and scenographical terms ('framing', 'staging', 'narrative'), but frequently we also see design strategies usually associated with theatre and performance in visual art, architecture, fashion and software design. Theatrical languages and methodologies are being adopted by architects, designers and visual artists to provide the frameworks for their creative practices, and it is clear that theatre design has increasing relevance and currency far outside its own traditional sphere.

However, few books on design theory and method look at theatre design. Among the exceptions is Norman Potter's classic text *What is a designer?*, first published in 1969. The author makes a brief acknowledgement of the 'complex design procedures' of theatre design but does not elaborate. John Chris Jones, another pioneer of design methodology, in his book on *Design Methods* (1970) identifies a new concern with the design of the 'total situation' and by the 1980 edition is recommending that designers learn about 'temporal design' from the 'time arts' including music, dance and theatre.

Theatre design as a discipline is expanding. At its broadest, scenography is the complete design of the performance environment, working with space, time, sound, costume, light, projection and narrative to visualize an experience that encompasses large-scale spectacles, intimate encounters and installations in both traditional and non-traditional theatre spaces.

These spaces offer ever increasing possibilities for designers for performance. Whether they choose to call themselves visual artists, sonic artists, architects, theatre designers, scenographers or performance designers – their contribution to the language of design theory is increasingly being acknowledged. This exhibition presents an opportunity to further

define and demonstrate a range of theatre design and practice. Through these examples, we learn about the process of designing: where ideas come from and how they become an event. These interviews examine what is meant by 'process'? Where does a process originate, how does it take shape and how is it maintained? What are the things that theatre designers do? We discover how ideas are developed or rejected in the process of experimentation in materials and making.

All of the designers included here acknowledge the processes of interaction and negotiation that define the objectives. In discussion with their collaborators – the directors, actors and technicians, lighting and sound designers, stage management – they identify and analyse potential problems, and their courses of action. They have to turn their own ideas and the ideas of their collaborators into physical objects and spaces. They both take and provide instructions, and must combine creative engineering with visual aesthetics.

The exhibitors demonstrate that their design process is not confined to the realization of one project, but is part of a conversation that develops across many projects. In the act of problem solving they may discover difficulties, but these are not seen as obstacles but as possibilities to explore new approaches to design. Garance Marneur, for example, describes how in *Khaos* (no.5) the initial idea of giving 'texture to the air' became a landscape of inflatables.

The designer needs to answer all the questions the performer has about their reality. Es Devlin (no.1) has described how she scans the text noting everything the actor has to touch – it has to be there on stage. Designers make experiences for both actors and audience to draw them into the other worlds. This may involve an exact and highly detailed interpretation of an actual place. For *Pasazerka* (no.20), for example, every element of Johan Engels's extraordinary set is based on the memories of the experiences of the author, Zofia Posmysz, formerly a prisoner in Auschwitz. Other designs might use very simple visual symbols to represent some abstract metaphorical location. As Naomi Wilkinson (no.13) observes, 'the steam from a boiling kettle' can be enough to establish the scene on an empty stage. Every aspect of these designs is carefully selected to support the narrative for performer and audience alike.

Costume is a fundamental element in the construction of the performance. Frames for the body are constructed in fabric, paper, and wood. Fotini Dimou notes that the manner in which the character Tekla was required to move in her full nineteenth-century corseted outfit was key to the decisions about the shape of her dress (no.19). Jamie Vartan's animated party dress for Violetta in *La Traviata* (no.12) is both a metaphorical and tangible representation of her mental and physical state. Costume does more than clothe the performer's body or give the character its identity. It is part of the entire scenic composition – it takes up space, it absorbs and reflects light, it creates visual texture and sound.

Representing Representation

Theatre design as a process is both systematic and spontaneous – a combination of imagination and calculation – and designers must be fluent in visual and verbal representation. Their procedures and processes require them to articulate not only their own ideas, but also the ideas of others. Drawings, models, photographs and words are the instruments, the tools, used to produce something, to know something, to measure it and to make it appear.

The 1:25 scale is the standard used widely in theatre design. It is the metric equivalent of the imperial measurement where an inch represented 1 foot, and is considered to provide the necessary level of detail and accuracy required by the theatre technicians, directors and actors to visualize (and realize) the final set. The aim of the model-maker is to create as 'real' or authentic a representation as possible, in order to test out the spatial relationships, structural arrangements, the positions and movement of bodies and objects, lighting effects and selection materials. While making the model, the maker is able to inhabit the space, to project him or herself into the scene.

7. (*below, left*)
The designer's desk by Ashley Shairp for the production *'Tis Pity She's a Whore*.

8. (*below, right*)
The designer's model by Johann Engels for the production *Pasazerka (The Passenger)*.

As Pippa Nissen observes 'you can get into the space, and start thinking about surface, quality of light, as well as space and form' (no.7). Michael Pavelka finds that by including scale figures of himself and the director, the model becomes 'real' (no.8).

Drawing, like modelling, is used in planning, detailing and working out key relationships – but it is also a visible record of process. Each designer has their own method and preferred media for particular tasks, from pencil sketches that storyboard initial concepts and activities, to expressive watercolours that illustrate atmosphere, character and costume. While Marie-Jeanne Lecca talks of thinking with a pencil (no.22), other designers use digital drawing, laser printing and visualization software to create animated storyboards, digital models and photoshopped images.

Whatever the technique, the process of making models and drawings allows designers to make changes, rethink, reinvent and reconstruct ideas. To the observer, the process may look messy and unorganized but the end result is a carefully considered and technically precise representation of an idea. This is imaginatively illustrated in Ashley Shairp's staging of the designer's desk (fig.7) to tell the story of the process of designing a production of 'Tis Pity She's a Whore (no.32).

Designers also experiment with the audience-performer relationship and their positioning in the space. They design in dialogue with the space, studying its acoustics, temperatures, smells, textures, visual and structural characteristics. They must plot sightlines and spatial dynamics between the performers and the audience to identify locations, positions and routes. They work in urban streets, remote landscapes, railway terminals and cathedrals, military training grounds, Cold War bunkers, museums, church halls – as well as theatres in the round, proscenium theatres, amphitheatres and arenas. But in all these spaces, the aim is to link audience and performance together, while communicating narrative.

This exhibition does not set out to replicate the original events, but aims instead to demonstrate the workings of the material and creative imagination (see fig.8). The exhibitors have chosen the images and objects they wish to represent their work; they are intended to illustrate the final outcomes, but also – and more importantly – to suggest their activities as designers. In their interviews a number of the designers stress the value of this documentation to their creative process. Models, drawings, workbooks, photographs, drawings and notes, sound recordings or videos are seen as inspiration for future activities as much as records of past events. Interestingly, while video is regarded as a useful resource for archival purposes and technical information, most of them seem to trust photography to be a more accurate representation of their work.

Hansjörg Schmidt describes the intention of the documented exhibit should be that it is 'a message in a bottle', a piece that arouses an emotional response in the viewer similar to that sought by the initial project (no.11). This is a view shared by many designers. Post Works re-present the idea of the performance using fragments from the original to create something new (no.9). In exhibiting their work, these designers reveal the passion, inventiveness and creativity that are inspiring and challenging audiences.

Each of these exhibitors has a distinct personal vision, but they also share contemporary aesthetics and preoccupations. There is in this work a romantic abstraction that combines the latest technologies with a strong sense of form and space and a sensual understanding of materiality and atmosphere. While references are often eclectic, the visual metaphors have a universality which triggers recognition and response. The designers' use of backcloths, gauzes and drops – hand-painted, laser-printed, projected, structural or sculptural – is notable, and evidence of a reinvigorated scenic tradition.

From Gormley to Gaga

Our selection ranges from Anthony Gormley's designs for dance (no.2) to Ralph Koltai's theatre designs for *An English Tragedy* (no.21) and on to Es Devlin's designs for Lady Gaga's *Monster Ball* tour (no.1). The exhibition includes British designers working overseas and international designers who have chosen to work in the creative environment of the UK. It represents innovation, is cross disciplinary, and reveals the variety and scale of projects produced over the last four years in performance design – from *La Boheme* in a village hall to stadium tours across the world.

War Horse, featured in this exhibition and designed by Rae Smith (no.33), has become a global phenomenon. Created at the National Theatre in London in 2007 the show has played to over a million people in London in the last four years and continues to capture the imagination of audiences around the world. The production was celebrated on Broadway in June 2011 winning five Tony Awards including Best Scenic Design of a Play. In the design Rae Smith's beautiful narrative sketch books are blown-up and presented on the stage as the landscape for the performance; in this exhibition they are displayed to illustrate the designer's working process and as beautiful objects in their own right.

The exhibition is an opportunity to trace the designers' collaborations and creative decisions, revealing how they create a production and their individual ways of recording and remembering that process. The exhibits become objects of study and each in turn deserves focus and investigation. We present the designs, often working tools for the designers, on open display and invite you to experience them up close.

The archives, galleries and spaces of the V&A are also a stage for site-specific performances, transformations and installations (fig.9). Designers and artists realize the beauty and the potential of the museum and its collections with fresh ideas and new interpretations. The contemporary designs for performance displayed at the V&A in 2012 connect the museum with current trends and practitioners and are part of a temporary touring exhibition programme which complements and enriches the permanent collection.

1. ES DEVLIN

Set designer

Monster Ball, World tour (2009–10)

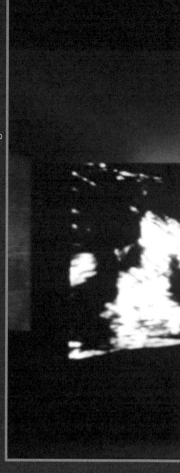

Images © Es Devlin

1. What influenced this work?

This particular project is slightly difficult to talk about, because it is of such a specific moment. One of the reasons Lady Gaga's visual work is so rich is because she is very involved in fashion. Nearly all her references come from fashion. We had a conversation with her for that tour when we were desperately late on the set. We knew if we didn't start building something that day, she wasn't going to have anything – and she started talking about the tights she was going to wear. I just said, 'Can we not talk about the tights, can we talk about the set design?' But she said, 'I have to understand what the tights are. And if I don't know what the shoes are, and if I don't know therefore what the dress is, and what the hat is, and the make-up is, then I don't know what space I need.'

I guess what you take away from that is, whatever you're going to build, make sure it's infinitely flexible so that it can adapt and mutate. And stay close to your artists, stay tuned-in because you can't try to think like they're thinking. You can't really resist it, because you do kind of sit there and think 'This goes back to my idea.' But that negates what their whole principle is, their whole nature of being this mercurial, constantly current quality. And as soon as you try to box them, even for a minute, then you're denying them what everyone else is actually celebrating about them, which is their absolute iconic being of the moment. And that's now and now and now and now, and not even ten minutes ago, which makes it very difficult to create.

2. Does your creative process begin and end with a performance, or is it a continuous development that transcends projects?

Well I think that it's really important to me to find a continuity throughout the whole. Particularly once you've had children, and the decision to go to work rather than be with your eighteen-month-old baby is a massive deal. If you're going to do it, you've got to be able to turn around after a passage of time and say, 'This constitutes a cumulative package of work.'

You can never predict a project. You might take it on and say, 'I'm going to be able to weave this in; I'm going to be able to use my past experience on this project.' But sometimes that just doesn't work, and at that point you have to go, 'Okay, I've still got a lot to glean from this.'

And then something might happen by accident, when people come into the studio and they see what's on the walls and go 'What's that?'. And these are things we're doing naturally. I really don't distinguish between Take That and *The Trojans*. I'm there. I see it all as one. If you're standing there with 80,000 people and they're all singing, I don't distinguish I'm afraid.

3. How important is the model as a visualization technique? How do you translate your designs into a performance space?

Well, the model – for me, I can't really live without it. And people keep saying to me, 'Do you really need it?' but I can't do without it – actually you need the model because you are making a piece of sculpture. I have started using 3D maps as well, because I've done a lot of straight lines in the past, and I really want to push myself to do these organic shapes that I've not done before. I just want to go there and see what happens – and trying to make them in model form is really hard. But for me the model is very important.

For dance in particular, you don't really design the show until you see what the moves are. And then you need to come in, and you give them a table, and then chop the table down – or maybe it needs to be a bit higher. And you have these conversations where, when you're designing for dance, the choreographer says something along the lines of 'I really like the feel of this bit here, and I need it to just come into my hip here.' You're almost doing a fitting with a piece of furniture.

4. What does performance design mean to you?

I've always seen it as something I'm doing at this point in my life, this point in my life being the last 15 years.

When I first started up I thought, 'I'll do this for now.' And the reason I wanted to do it then was that I wanted to draw and to collaborate. I wanted what I made to be made in collaboration. And I felt that the ideas came, and still come, when in conversation. And that's how it works. When the director is sitting there, or now with other designers, because I'm working much more with associates, that's when the ideas actually happen.

I trust that process so much that now that when I go into a meeting with a director I'll just 'glean', and have my antennae out, and pick up on what they're

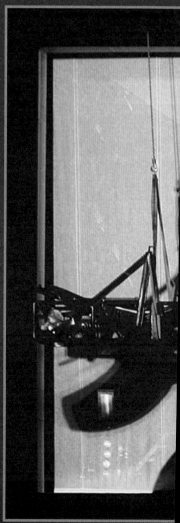

saying. I just think about what we're going to make, and I don't make anything on my own. There isn't, really, at any moment, a sense of what I want to do. And for me, that's the best way (this probably sounds quite pretentious), just to be alive. I think, even when I started, that I would produce richer work in collaboration.

You know that sense you get that you're having a really good idea? Or you look at a colleague, and you know they're going to have a really good idea? Well that happens. It's a by-product of having a great conversation with someone. And just how it feels when you're having a fantastic conversation. That moment of sitting with a colleague and having a great conversation and coming up with a great idea – that, for me, is where I feel most happy and creative. I think that's why I design for performance as opposed to anything else.

5. Is it important to document performance?
I'm really obsessive about documenting my work compared to a lot of people I work with. I photograph everything. Usually three times. There are some shows I don't manage to get because circumstances are really tricky, and it seems a bit naff to get your camera out. I just started re-doing my website with video, and I haven't put it online because I'm now really careful about how I edit video. My experience of the shows is in the photos. They are selected moments of how I want you to see the show, and how I want to remember the show myself.

In the photos to some degree I can wrest back control of the story of what happens on stage. Of course I will collaborate with every last bone in my body while the show is still being cooked, and do everything I can to make every moment a moment that I'm proud of. But in the end, I will select those moments. And oddly enough, because we're not making specifically for film, in a way I think the least good way to appreciate a theatre performance is to watch a film of it. Unless – maybe – if it was set up being considered as a film when the performance happens.

You might say that the photograph doesn't tell you what it feels like to be there, but that's not really what I'm trying to do. The photograph is me showing you that photograph. The photograph for me is an object in itself.

2. ANTONY GORMLEY

Scenographer

Sutra (A Sadler's Wells London Production)

Sadler's Wells, London (May 2008)

1. What influenced this work?
Shoe boxes, sentry boxes, pill boxes, cupboards, coffins, chests, boats, baths, hiding holes, graves, beds, cells, rooms, seas, deserts, cities.

2. Does your creative process begin and end with a performance, or is it a continuous development that transcends projects?
Experimentation, confrontation, connection, contemplation.

3. How important is the model as a visualization technique? How do you translate your designs into a performance space?
Making toys and playing with them at all scales.

4. What does performance design mean to you?
Another body for the action to evolve with.

5. Is it important to document performance?
There is no way to objectively record the actuality of dance: you can involve filming within the dance, and get a uniquely integrated – but particular – view.

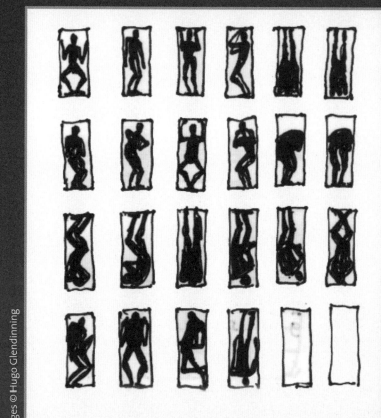

Images © Hugo Glendinning

3. RICHARD HUDSON

Set and costume designer
Rushes – Fragments of a Lost Story,
Royal Opera House, London (April 2008)

1. What influenced this work?
The narrative of the ballet was based loosely on an episode in Dostoevsky's *The Idiot*, and the music was composed by Prokofiev in 1936 for an unfinished film. The choreographer, Kim Brandstrup, and I started by looking at Russian paintings and photographs of that period – Meyerhold, Mayakovsky and the Constructivists. The costumes ended up being a bit more 1920s in feel, the colours came from portraits by Modigliani, and the main protagonist's costume from a photograph of the poet Boris Pasternack wearing a thick jumper.

2. Does your creative process begin and end with a performance, or is it a continuous development that transcends projects?
The creative process is continuously developing, from the start of the first meeting with the choreographer or director, right up to the curtain going up on the opening night. My inspiration comes chiefly from collaboration and research.

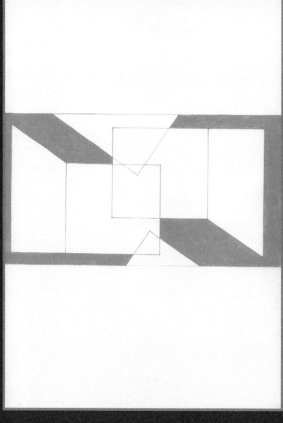

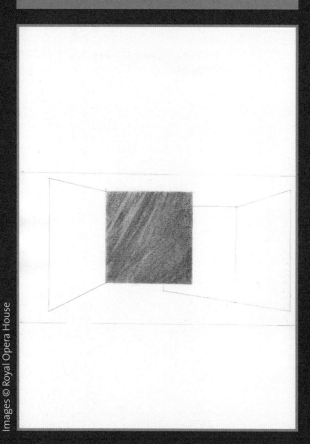

Images © Royal Opera House

3. How important is the model as a visualization technique? How do you translate your designs into a performance space?
For me, three-dimensional models are vital. I can't work on a computer. The models we make in my studio look exactly like the set will appear on stage, only 25 times smaller. It's important to be able to appraise the quality of the space, even in a smaller scale.

4. What does performance design mean to you?
Performance design is supporting a cast and director in the telling of a story, and making it look 'wonderful'.

5. Is it important to document performance?
I think it is important that good work should be documented or recorded in some way, however far that may be from the real thing. But I do love the ethereality of theatre – now you see it, now you don't.

I DO LOVE THE ETHEREALITY OF THEATRE
– NOW YOU SEE IT, NOW YOU DON'T

1. What influenced this work?

The first impression of the space is always the main influence. How does it feel to be in the space? Who is using it? What is its history? The architecture of the new Ashmolean Museum extension and the beautiful layout of the objects in the space were very inspiring.

2. Does your creative process begin and end with a performance, or is it a continuous development that transcends projects?

Each project that I work on I see as a unique process, it is only when I'm asked to talk about my work that I begin to see patterns and preoccupations that transcend projects. Through teaching I have also begun to identify my design 'method'. Susanne Thomas, the Artistic Director of the seven sisters group, and I bounce ideas off each other, do a lot of research and then continue to experiment in the space, refining over and over until we have a performance.

3. How important is the model as a visualization technique? How do you translate your designs into a performance space?

I do not use models in the site-specific work I do with seven sisters group. The pieces are often a journey, and the specifics of the journey are not always defined until quite late in the process. In recent years I have rarely changed the space; it has been more about responding to the space and finding the locations/positions for the audience and performers that give a new experience or viewpoint of the environment. I also rarely create drawings or costume designs in this kind of work. I will do a lot of research when we are planning the project and the themes, and then I try out costumes and props and change them as we go along.

4. What does performance design mean to you?

It means variety: new challenges, new experiences and new things to find out about. A combination of movement, sound, text, light and the 'design/ scenography' that can convey very powerful ideas and emotions.

5. Is it important to document performance?

It is very important to document the performance. In the work that we do, the run of a show may only be a week, and the audience numbers quite limited. Although you can never capture the live experience, you can capture some of its spirit. Video appears to capture more detail, but I think photographs are more expressive.

ALTHOUGH YOU CAN NEVER CAPTURE THE LIVE
EXPERIENCE OF ATTENDING A PERFORMANCE,
YOU CAN CAPTURE SOME OF ITS SPIRIT

5. GARANCE MARNEUR

Set and costume designer

Khaos, Scottish Dance Theatre and UK tour (2010/11)

1. What influenced this work?

Khaos started with the idea of personifying or giving texture to the air – along with the themes of deprivation and excess. Exploring the world of inflatables was interesting in terms of the interaction the dancers could have with them, but also as a landscape because we could quickly reshape the dynamic of the space. We also took inspiration from Khaos, the Greek goddess of air: from nothing, she created everything. Her name is also used to describe a state of utter confusion or disorder, and we aimed to use the inflatables to morph and constantly evolve.

PERFORMANCE DESIGN FOR ME IS VISUALIZING AND CREATING A WORLD IN WHICH THE CHARACTERS CAN LIVE AND EVOLVE

  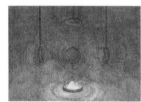  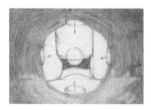

2. Does your creative process begin and end with a performance, or is it a continuous development that transcends projects?

Each project wants to have its own identity. From selecting materials to the realization on stage, there exists a sort of beginning and end. However, it never feels like the work is finished. While making so many discoveries throughout the process, you also make choices, and some unused ideas might be used in future productions when the opportunities arise. In that respect, I can say that my design investigations transcend projects. My creativity takes me on a journey with my collaborators, and on *Khaos*, the unpredictable nature of the inflatables means that we always end in a different place.

3. How important is the model as a visualization technique? How do you translate your designs into a performance space?

The model is – most of the time – my 'bible' from start to finish. It helps to communicate your ideas visually with the team, and it gives an overview of the space and informs the build. I usually start with a sketch model, often in 1:50 scale, that I can carry around with me and transform easily, but it is not always possible; with *Khaos*, for instance, it made more sense to experiment with the actual inflatable.

I always consider the relationship between body and space in my projects. What is the journey of the characters? Is the world they live in supporting them? Is there an obstacle, or a threat, looming over the scene? Should the set be functional and interactive, or an 'environment'? Looking at those questions tells me what the production needs from the design.

4. What does performance design mean to you?

Performance design for me is visualizing and creating a world in which the characters can live and evolve. It often feels important to remain true to an original idea without forgetting that the more simple and strong it is, the better. Performance design also allows me to explore various disciplines and topics, with new writing or classical texts with a modern relevance.

6. CONOR MURPHY

Set and costume designer

The Magic Flute, National Opera of Korea (March 2009)

SCENERY IS ONLY USEFUL IF IT ENHANCES
WHAT IS HAPPENING BETWEEN THE
PERFORMERS

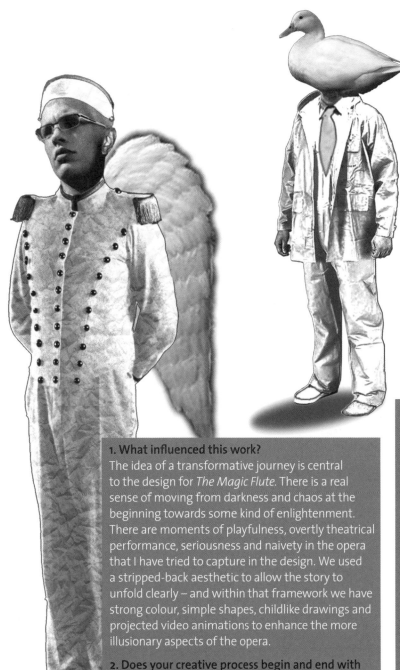

Images © Conor Murphy

1. What influenced this work?

The idea of a transformative journey is central
to the design for *The Magic Flute*. There is a real
sense of moving from darkness and chaos at the
beginning towards some kind of enlightenment.
There are moments of playfulness, overtly theatrical
performance, seriousness and naivety in the opera
that I have tried to capture in the design. We used
a stripped-back aesthetic to allow the story to
unfold clearly – and within that framework we have
strong colour, simple shapes, childlike drawings and
projected video animations to enhance the more
illusionary aspects of the opera.

2. Does your creative process begin and end with a performance, or is it a continuous development that transcends projects?

It is a collaboration that begins in the first
conversation with the director and continues until
the first performance when our contract ends!
Working more than once with the same team can
sometimes allow us to develop ideas that may have
started in previous projects. Experimentation is
more likely when a degree of trust has developed
between the collaborators.

3. How important is the model as a visualization technique? How do you translate your designs into a performance space?

A model is an indispensable tool in discussions
with the director, as it tends to evolve during
our meetings. I try to keep the process as fluid
as possible so that we arrive at something that
is a unique result of our collaboration. This can
sometimes mean tearing things up and completely
reorganizing the space during a meeting.

4. What does performance design mean to you?

Through design we can somehow influence the
emotional journey of a piece. Scenery is only useful
if it enhances what is happening between the
performers. I have always been interested in the
spatial dynamics between the performers and
how we respond to that as an audience. In the
early stages of the design I try to visualize these key
relationships in quick sketches, and the space often
develops around that.

5. Is it important to document performance?

DVDs are the most practical document if the
production is to be revived or transferred. They
rarely show the performance at its best, but it
is great to have films of performances that you
couldn't see live.

7. PIPPA NISSEN

Set and costume designer

Elephant and Castle, Aldeburgh Music Festival,
Snape Maltings, Suffolk (June 2007)

1. What influenced this work?

We were lucky enough to have an extended period of collaboration for this project, spanning three years. It started as an Arts Council Research and Development award and then, once the Aldeburgh Festival of Music and the Arts got involved, became an extended series of workshops. This was a rich working relationship with the two composers (Mira Calix and Tansy Davies), writer (Blake Morrison), director (Tim Hopkins), lighting designer (Zerlina Hughes) and myself. Each of us brought reams of research to the table, which we collated and drew on in the workshops as we tightened up the performance and narrative possibilities.

We were interested in exploring the idea of putting one place into another, and looking at all the friction and excitement that resulted from the juxtapositions. I was (and still am) interested in how spaces and places can change, and so I wanted the surfaces and forms to be able to transform in some way. For the set I wanted a poetic blankness – something that seemed able to tell a story without being too prescriptive.

We spent a long time researching the local area around Snape Maltings where the Aldeburgh Festival is held, and also the Elephant and Castle area in London. We wanted to look at how two moments of 1960s architectural optimism led to the birth of two new 'complete' worlds in which the architect's vision was paramount – the Elephant and Castle Shopping Centre and the Aldeburgh Music buildings at Snape Maltings.

At the time Elephant and Castle shopping centre was revolutionary, an indoor space with lots of shops under one roof. There were fountains and artwork – a futuristic ideal of life. We found local newspapers that had hailed it as one of London's top three destinations for tourists, and linked it to the new cultural quarter on the Southbank. Aldeburgh was undergoing a development of a different kind, a new music school and auditorium developed by Benjamin Britten and others, and in their world the architect's vision catered for all aspects of a student's creative life; it was meant to inspire and transform. The two projects were supposed to be all encompassing.

We also spent a long time documenting everything. Snape Maltings was undergoing a building programme, so we filmed the buildings being destroyed over several months. We also recorded different routes through the Elephant and Castle.

THE CREATIVE
PROCESS IS NEVER
SIMPLE AND HAS
NO RULES

2. Does your creative process begin and end with a performance, or is it a continuous development that transcends projects?

The creative process is never easy and has no rules. What works for one project doesn't for the next. Generally we start with a brainstorm, casting the net as wide as possible. Through editing the ideas get explored and refined. I think that the good projects lead me to somewhere completely different, where the collaborative team teases out a new story by building on everyone's strengths. It shouldn't ever be over. At some point you have to freeze the designs, because of the practical constraints of tendering and building the work, which is frustrating. There are always the last-minute touches that make a huge difference, that add the specific details that come out of rehearsals, or even performances. For me the fuels of creativity are the collaboration and the research – the enjoyment of discussion, and the excitement of working with interesting people who have different specialist areas.

3. How important is the model as a visualization technique? How do you translate your designs into a performance space?

I rely on a physical model for designing my work. For me, it is not only a natural way to visualize the work, but also an essential basis for discussion with the creative team as a whole. I enjoy the 1:25 scale that scene models are made in – it's larger than most of the models we make for my architectural practice. It means that you can 'think' into the space, and start looking at surface or the quality of light, as well as space and form. I always use cutout figures; they provide the all-important human scale.

We always model our work on the computer as well, as this is a useful way of moving through the spaces from someone's viewpoint, and seeing how the spaces might change.

We also use a perspective view, or collage, and sketching alongside models. They all provide a different way to test ideas and they communicate different things – from the broad brush to detail.

4. What does performance design mean to you?

As I also work on architectural projects and exhibition design, for me performance design can be much more playful and experimental. We think of it in the studio as a test-bed of ideas for the longer-lasting work in my architectural projects. The theatre designs are all about how people use space, and how space can transform into lots of different things. That is what I am constantly trying to capture in my buildings – which become the backdrop to people's lives. I am also interested in how space can become a way of exploring a narrative, or a way of suggesting a story that gets completed in your imagination. How an idea can be abstracted and mean more than one thing.

5. Is it important to document performance?

This is a huge problem for me – sometimes it feels as if in the long run the project is only as good as the photos you take! I have learnt from this at last, and now bring in photographers to shadow my work for a few days (and therefore get the right images). It's difficult to remember to do this; as a production gets nearer, you're so busy that getting a photographer is the last thing on your mind. Once the project has finished, and the years pass, certain images become important, and I now know each production through one or two moments that capture the essence of the piece. I have filmed performances, but for me these never show the quality of work.

I have one or two photographers that I trust to know what interests me. For *Elephant and Castle* there was a huge electrical storm during the dress rehearsal – when we would have normally taken the more staged photos. The whole cast and crew sat in the bar and watched as the wind and rain took over the landscape. It meant that all the photos were taken during the first performance, and so only a small amount of shots were taken, but they are all very atmospheric and of the moment.

Images © Aldburgh Music

1. What influenced this work?

The site inspired me and others in the team to devise a human story on an epic architectural canvas. We collected, swapped and amalgamated stories: E.M. Forster's *The Machine Stops* made a huge impression on me as a teenager, so that featured. We were driven by contrasting the mass of buildings with the weightlessness of a performer.

2. Does your creative process begin and end with a performance, or is it a continuous development that transcends projects?

'Creative process' seems like the wrong way to think about it. It's a struggle – I lurch from one project to the next not knowing if I can ever bring myself to do another production. Fear. I try to start afresh with each one as if I feel as if it's my first (or last) show, and I'll terrify myself into starting. Responsibility and responding to others is another incentive – I imagine how the design will support a particular group effort. Making any piece of theatre is a small miracle.

3. How important is the model as a visualization technique? How do you translate your designs into a performance space?

I've become less and less convinced by models, but directors like them. I can't stand making them any more; they frustrate and anger me. I had no physical model for *Off the Wall*, I drew traditionally and then worked with the artistic and technical teams to realize the design on-site. The space was so large, a model wouldn't have come close to describing the audience's immersive experience. We used computers to work out the engineering. When I do use a model I first make a scale figure of myself and the director – we are standing in front of it – then it becomes 'real'. I am 'talking' to the director, discussing what we see … it's mad but it's a trick I have to play with myself – it stops me from treating the model as a doll's house.

4. What does performance design mean to you?

Thinking about a complete event – shaping and sharing a vision.

5. Is it important to document performance?

It's important for me to go through the motions. I'm getting better at it, and even becoming a bit obsessive. I know it's important because recently I thought I had lost my production folder in a hotel just after the show had opened and got into a genuine panic, but having said that, once it's bound up in a book of documents, images and publicity, it's of little real use to me. Why is it important? I may have an arrogant belief that someone else might be interested – my children maybe? Photographs still outstrip a moving recording, because stills don't compete with the live experience but suspend moments in equally poignant ways. This exhibit is a collage.

STILLS DON'T COMPETE WITH THE LIVE EXPERIENCE BUT SUSPEND MOMENTS IN EQUALLY POIGNANT WAYS

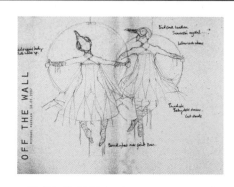

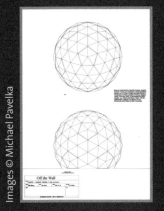

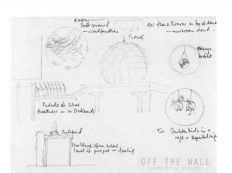

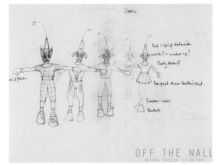

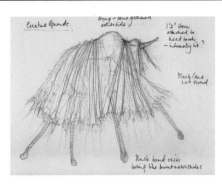

9. POST WORKS

Set designers

Stage City/Lapped Translated Lines,
Riverside Studios, London (November 2008)

1. What influenced this work?

Central to all our work is the idea of the city as a stage set, and how this can change the way we inhabit and think about architecture and the city.

Buildings and urban spaces influence our movement and behaviour in both deliberate and unexpected ways, and once you start to notice how the city really impacts on us, in a cultural and social sense, it can become quite disturbing. This was central to the work *Stage City*, a fictional performance-city machine staged inside a glass vitrine that borrowed familiar elements from London to create an assemblage of characters, props and sets. Steps, ramps and routes – designed and improvised performance spaces – were sampled and edited to create a familiar landscape, but one that was rearranged and re-imagined, appearing as a well-oiled city-machine with a logic different from that which we're used to experiencing.

2. Does your creative process begin and end with a performance, or is it a continuous development that transcends projects?

It's a continuous development across projects. Our work and ideas are fuelled by a collaborative process between ourselves and the other artists we work with. It gives energy to all the projects we do. We hand over aspects of projects to other people to develop and then respond to the work produced; that way unexpected things can happen.

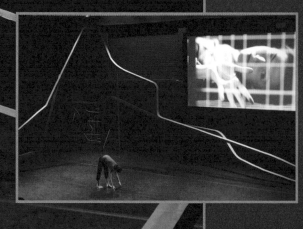

Images © Tim Brotherton

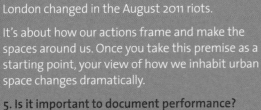

3. How important is the model as a visualization technique? How do you translate your designs into a performance space?
We use different types of modelling at different stages, sometimes physical and sometimes on computer. The designs we work on move constantly between these different modes of representation – and we draw. Each stage will change what we are proposing as we incorporate the discrepancies each medium allows. It's important for us to use the gaps and changes of direction that emerge from every iteration of a piece of work.

On several occasions we have moved directly from the 'sketch model' into the final object – the fabricator working directly from our first intuitive act.

4. What does performance design mean to you?
Cities are basically places that frame, control or enable events, and performances take place in everyday situations. It's interesting how an act can be recorded into the fabric of a city. Look at the way London changed in the August 2011 riots.

It's about how our actions frame and make the spaces around us. Once you take this premise as a starting point, your view of how we inhabit urban space changes dramatically.

5. Is it important to document performance?
The documentation of a performance should almost be seen as a very different piece of work. To try to recreate something that is experienced as an event is futile. We always treat our documentation with both complete respect and – at the same time – total scepticism. For this reason most of our performance stills are taken outside of the actual performances, with photographers, film-makers and editors that have no particular relationship to the theatre, performance or architecture.

10. KATHRINE SANDYS

Sonic Artist/Scenographer

Hush House, RAF Bentwaters, near Woodbridge, Suffolk (March 2010)

1. What influenced this work?

Hush House was truly site-specific in that the inspiration for the manifestation of sound came purely from the space. The overall project started with the Bentwaters Royal Air Force site itself. As children, my brother and I visited it in active service, but we only ever saw it through a chain link fence, at the end of the runway.

We visited RAF Bentwaters, now known as Bentwaters Parks, for a research trip to finally see the peculiar buildings and objects we couldn't access during the Cold War. Our associations and memories of the Cold War, given to us through novels and films, inspired the work as an experience – the journey to the site, the anticipation of what the work would be and then the revelation of a very alien space. I wanted to capture the epic, romantic adventure that Cold War is often portrayed as, when it's shown through mediated documents.

The visceral experience of the sound of the building had to be present to highlight its purpose and bring it to life – distinct from our more general memories of the Cold War. It was the feel of the sound in the space that really animated it and captured the audience's imaginations – regardless of whether they had any tangible connections to our memories of the Cold War.

2. Does your creative process begin and end with a performance, or is it a continuous development that transcends projects?

Hush House is a good example of what drives my creative process: it is about making some sort of connection that feels tangible enough to be personal for anyone. For me, the sensory experience is the most direct way to do this, which is why light and sound are my preferred media. The wavelengths of either are what I play with as tools and, without sounding too sinister, it is the memory of their penetration of the body that is the experience the audience takes away.

I enjoy the experimentation that solo work enables, but I sometimes miss the collaboration of a great team – when the project involves others that you have a great respect for it can really help fuel your own creative imagination. There is nothing like seeing something exciting emerge from a series of individual ideas. It is thrilling when that kind of dialogue exists within a creative team.

3. How important is the model as a visualization technique? How do you translate your designs into a performance space?

The thing about sound and light, of course, is that they are not tangible, and therefore one of the hardest things is to present an audio or visual model in advance. I use as many devices as possible, including objects, colours, emotions, or even smells, but often very descriptive language is the most important thing. Research is vital, and this can present a healthy amount of imagery that at least paints a picture of the world I am trying to create. Drawings and technical diagrams can help to work out calculations, but they can also be alienating when I'm collaborating with other people as they can look like a private code.

The relationship between body and space is central to my initial concepts and therefore, hopefully, also to the final event. The audience is the most important component of the work as it is their experience they will be taking away, both as the work, and as the memory of the work. I always consider how they will engage with the work on a physiological, emotional and intellectual level.

4. What does performance design mean to you?

The word 'scenography' has been unfashionable in the UK for the last 30 years, but it's the perfect description of what performance design is: a complete fabricated environment that supports and tells the story. This works right across the range of live performance, from huge concert spectacles through to site-specific installations. Even a site-specific work with no apparent design intervention is still a considered space, and has been considered for all its visual and acoustic properties. Scenography is the craft of using whatever devices are available to create the desired environment – sound, light, costume, props, film, surfaces or structures. I consider myself a scenographer, and am pleased to see the word re-emerging in our language as a way of describing someone who constructs an environment.

Images © Sam Heath

Images © Simon Sandys

Images © Sam Heath

5. Is it important to document performance?
Performance documentation is a paradox. Live performance engages with an audience in a different way from recorded media, and this makes documentation of live work very difficult; it is never the same experience as a first-hand encounter. *Hush House* is a work not just about the experience of the immersive environment and the journey to that site – it also uses sound frequencies below human audible level, only experienced through the sensation they create in the body. It is this sensation that creates the sense of presence of the building. These frequencies of sound could never be captured by a recording device, and would need to be played back in an exact replica of the original space in order to come anywhere close to a true representation of the original work. This visceral engagement is lost in the work's documentation and yet, without the document, there is only the memory of the work.

Hush House is presented as a document of the work, but is edited in a contrived way to make an alternative piece of work, not a representation of the original. The debate about recording performance will no doubt go on for a long time.

11. HANSJÖRG SCHMIDT
Lighting designer

Kursk, Young Vic, London (June 2009)

1. What influenced this work?

This was a highly collaborative creative process, so all ideas came out of the 12-month Research and Development period before the production. The highly structured nature of everyday life on a submarine provided inspiration, as did my general interest in using light as a dramaturgical tool to bind a piece (production and audience) together.

2. Does your creative process begin and end with a performance, or is it a continuous development that transcends projects?

I see this definitely as a continuous development, with collaboration very much at the centre of things, supported by research. Lighting a show without acknowledging and developing what has gone before would generate reductive and repetitive work. Research is central, and allows the practitioner to actively move their discipline forward.

3. How important is the model as a visualization technique? How do you translate your designs into a performance space?

Designs are developed through lots of meetings and research. Often the key moment is the choice of an appropriate lighting language – in this case the use of the LED striplights to delineate the set and express the 'foreignness' of the ship's architecture.

Images © Keith Pattison

PERFORMANCE SPACE MUST INCLUDE CONSIDERATION OF THE AUDIENCE'S ROLE, AND THE SPACE THEY INHABIT

4. What does performance design mean to you?
I think performance design is key to any text (verbal or non-verbal) put before an audience; without it there can be no shared space and no meaningful dialogue. For this to take place, a space needs to be chosen and defined. The choice may be a white box, or a recreation of Wienerwald (the woods outside Vienna). Crucially, performance space must include consideration of the role of the audience, and the space they inhabit.

5. Is it important to document performance?
It is important to document performance, but I don't think we have found the right way to do this yet. Maybe the best option is to document through small versions of larger events: the documented show as a message in a bottle. What I mean by that is the creation of a piece that tries to trigger an emotional response similar to the initial project's aims. So, as an example, for *Kursk* it might be listening to the sound of water in total blackness.

12. JAMIE VARTAN

Set and costume designer

La Traviata, Malmo Opera, Sweden
(December 2008)

1. What influenced this work?
The starting point was Violetta's illness. Tuberculosis has been romanticized, and it is said to produce feelings of euphoria and bursts of energy in the last moments before death; the sufferer is drowned from within, water filling their lungs. We needed to make a link between drowning and euphoria.

The slow motion video footage of Violetta fully clothed and falling into a swimming pool provided an instinctive and direct link to the hugely influential music. The dress fabric and air bubbles in the water made lives of their own, defying gravity. Her floating party dress described the character as much as her own body did.

2. Does your creative process begin and end with a performance, or is it a continuous development that transcends projects?
Processes from past and present productions always overlap and feed each other. Inspiration for experimentation comes from authenticity, and from constantly listening to and observing everyday life – everyday characters; hearing someone relay to you a moving or life changing story; news events; how people are reacting; what experiences people are having. You're looking for strong juxtapositions.

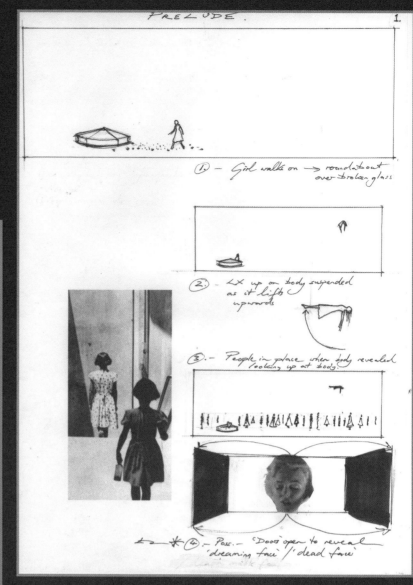

Images © Malin Arnesson

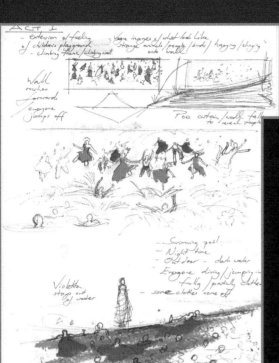

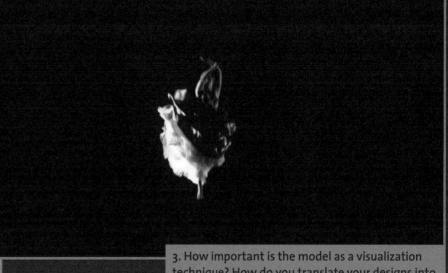

PERFORMANCE DESIGN ... PROVIDES THE OPPORTUNITY TO BE SELECTIVE, TO FOCUS AN AUDIENCE ON A PARTICULAR JOURNEY

3. How important is the model as a visualization technique? How do you translate your designs into a performance space?

The model provides a good means of communication and can inspire other collaborators. An initial visit to the performance space is crucial, to establish the scale of the performers and their relationship both to the audience and to the space around them. Then straight to sketching continuously, all as creative 'food' prior to starting the model.

I spend a lot of time imagining the model at full scale, imagining seeing it in the workshop, in the rehearsal room, on stage. Its weight. Its feel. Its texture. Then you look around at similar scale constructions and textures that you can find, in the street or landscapes or interiors. You want to see how people are in scale to them.

4. What does performance design mean to you?

When we listen to a performance on the radio or with our eyes closed, we all have – to some extent – numerous fixed 'designs' that comes in to our heads.

Performance design, when the boundaries between direction and design appear seamless, provides the opportunity to be selective, to focus an audience on a particular journey while still allowing (and provoking) countless new directions.

5. Is it important to document performance?

Archives help to provide an understanding of how current work sits in the context of a body of work. A thorough production video, with a number of cameras, comes into its own when mounting a revival, providing as much information as possible necessary for the production team. However, archived research material or an evocative archived storyboard can provide far more inspiration, as the source of the production once again feels alive.

13. NAOMI WILKINSON

Set and costume designer

La Dispute, Abbey Theatre, Dublin (2008–9)

1. What influenced this work?
I was attracted by the notion of deceit. There is unease that accompanies our pleasure when we watch the antics of animals in a zoo, which stems from the poverty of their simulated natural environment. I wanted something of that on stage.

The play is set at the point when four adolescents confined since birth are allowed to meet for the first time. The rough sliding doors suggest the hidden enclosures in which up until then they have dwelt, while the space they have been 'freed' into is clearly and cruelly a closed pen, there for the entertainment of the onlookers. The printed forest walls serve as a cipher for the deception wrought on the children, who will have never seen the real thing, and so would know no better.

2. Does your creative process begin and end with a performance, or is it a continuous development that transcends projects?
Each project brings its own variables and unique challenges, but I see my work as one ongoing process that is mutated by the individual productions, some of whose fragments reappear and fuel further works.

Images © Naomi Wilkinson

ON AN EMPTY STAGE, THE STEAM FROM A BOILING KETTLE MIGHT BE ENOUGH TO SET THE SCENE

3. How important is the model as a visualization technique? How do you translate your designs into a performance space?

Rather than trying to translate imagined images that I have drawn, I render my ideas in three dimensions almost immediately, making a scale model that can be manipulated. I use the actual materials that will form the set from the start in the model, to see how they will play and so fine tune the space with the director. Later I photograph the model and storyboard the scenes, which in some respects returns the ideas to two dimensions. Many people find that more comprehensible.

4. What does performance design mean to you?

It could be anything that works. On an empty stage, the steam from a boiling kettle might be enough to set the scene.

5. Is it important to document performance?

Perhaps it really isn't possible to document performance, but documents made of performance are both inspirational and a necessary resource.

14. SIMON BANHAM
Designer

The Persians, Sennybridge Training Area (August 2010)

Images © Simon Banham

Our production was held at Sennybridge Training Area (called 'SENTA'), a Ministry of Defence training area in the Brecon Beacons, in a mock village called 'FIBUA' (or Fighting In Built Up Areas) that was built for soldiers to simulate house-to-house fighting. SENTA is an area required to be 'potentially anywhere', and we were in a place used to rehearse for real events that would take place elsewhere. Our occupation, therefore, was designed to be as congruent as possible with the site; these structures were built for 'performance', for the observation and understanding of actions.

15. DONATELLA BARBIERI
Set and costume designer

Encounters in the Archive,
The Victoria and Albert Museum, London

Encounters in the Archive used the V&A Theatre and Performance Archive as its scenographic space, and the stored and conserved costumes as characters. We took the costumes out of their acid-free storage, and filmed 'encounters' between them and six artists, designers and writers. These included costume designer Nicky Gillibrand (who met Giorgio De Chirico and Mikhail Larionov's costumes); author Amy de la Haye (who responded to Chanel and Beaton); fashion designer Darren Cabon (who met with Victorian clowns), and artist Charlotte Hodes (who encountered eighteenth-century *ballet de court* costumes).

Images © Donatella Barbieri

16. PAUL BROWN

Set and costume designer

Aida, Bregenz Festival, Austria (July 2009)

Image © Stuart Nunn

Image © Karl Forster

During the final Triumphant March, cranes lifted the various parts of the submerged head out of the water to create the complete face. Simultaneously, the torch was raised from the bottom of the lake. The cranes become vehicles of both the construction, and the deconstruction, of 'Liberty Enlightening the World'. Mechanical – and therefore inevitable – they were intended to operate like Fate.

17. CHARLIE CRIDLAN

Set and costume designer

La Boheme, Wedmore Opera, Somerset (July 2008)

Images © Tessa Podpadeck

This production was real transformation. I designed compound rakes, auditorium and stage, which created a wonderful new acoustic in the turn-of-the-century village hall. The space felt epic, but with an amazing intimacy, and gave the audience the sensation of floating on air. There was a walkway – complete with delicate ironwork – that surrounded the orchestra, and we included a selection of posters from 1880s Paris that helped to frame the interior scenes, and extend those set outside.

18. BOB CROWLEY

Set designer

The Year of Magical Thinking, National Theatre, London (March 2007)

Images © Brigitte Lacombe

The design consisted of six paintings on silk that charted the character's journey to the heart of grief following the sudden death of her husband. I thought of them as six 'landscapes of grief'.

19. FOTINI DIMOU / BEN STONES

Costume / Set designer

Creditors, Donmar Warehouse, London and Harvey Theatre, New York (2008)

Fotini Dimou, Costume Designer
The way Tekla moved in her nineteenth-century corseted outfit was key to our decisions about the shape of her dress. The steel-grey central panel of her dress was meant to be like her armour. She looks all buttoned up and sharp, but we lined the outfit in a deep red fabric that is just visible around her neckline and on the inside of her cuffs; this was meant as a subtle hint of frivolity and femininity.

Ben Stones, Set Designer
The director's note to me was that the room should feel like a Louise Bourgeois sculptured creature. I interpreted this with a mix of organic materials (wood and water) teamed with metal girders that gave the space a cold, clinical and uninviting feel. The room sat on a vast pit filled with water, with the legs that supported the room disappearing into the murky depths. A threatening, but beautiful, room.

Images © Hugo Glendinning

20. JOHAN ENGELS

Set designer

Pasazerka (The Passenger), Bregenz Festival, Austria (July 2010)

Images © Karl Forster

Pasazerka (The Passenger) by the Polish-Russian composer Mieczysław Weinberg was rediscovered by David Pountney before its first performance at the Bregenz Festival in 2010. The author of the semi-autobiographical novel that the opera is based on, Zofia Posmysz, spent four years as a prisoner in Auschwitz and worked very closely with us in production. It is a powerful piece set simultaneously on a 1960s passenger line and the concentration camp. Although it is impossible to represent Auschwitz and its horrors on stage, every detail of the set had to be an exact memory of Zofia's experiences.

21. RALPH KOLTAI

Set designer

An English Tragedy, Palace Theatre, Watford (February 2008)

The subject of Ronald Harwood's play is the traitor John Amery, who broadcast to Britain on behalf of Hitler's Third Reich during the Second World War. He was tried for treason by a British Court, found guilty and executed by Albert Pierrepoint at Wandsworth Prison in December 1946.

Images © Ralph Koltai

22. MARIE-JEANNE LECCA

Costume designer

Agrippina, Opernhaus Zurich (May 2009)

I think best with a pencil. The costume drawing is, for me, absolutely crucial in delivering the conceptual details regarding the identity of the characters, firstly to the director and other members of the creative team, and, finally, to the makers. It enables the process of transformation from imagination to reality, from two dimensions to three, and should also tell the story.

Images © Suzanne Schwiertz

23. VERENA LEO

Set and costume designer

QUaRteT, Robin Howard Theatre, London (June 2008)

Images © Verena Leo

QUaRteT was performed twice, as two different versions. For the first, I joined the choreographer quite late in the artistic process, and my design was shaped by the movements that had already developed. I found that constant drawing was essential to helping me understand and know the choreography.

I explored domestic themes and spaces, and added hanging chairs and a kitchen table that suddenly put the four female dancers into a context that gave the movements new meaning. Strengthened by the lighting, and without being overly realistic, the space gained depth and impact. The piece grew through the feeling of wanting to burst, break out and expand space in all directions, and keeping one of the stage doors open during the entire performance enforced this sense of necessary escape.

For the second version, almost a year later, we integrated a white backdrop into the performance. We tried to redefine the piece without losing what we initially aimed for and, I think, finally highlighted the dark essence of the piece even more.

24. JOHN MACFARLANE

Set and costume designer

Cinderella, Birmingham Royal Ballet (November 2010)

From the outset we knew that we wanted it to be quite a dark version of the fairy tale, where you remember that the story is actually about the abuse of the young Cinderella. Because of that we thought very seriously about how to portray certain scenes. For example, at the beginning, when we are in the kitchen, you want a level of realism – so there was no point in having a kitchen fill the entire stage. You need it to be on a realistic scale and you need to really get the impression of Cinderella as totally abused and downtrodden.

Designing for classical ballet is much more difficult than some other genres especially when it is a big three act production. It is the sheer logistics. You have all these ideas but then they have to fit into the grid and the size of the stage. You have an idea, and that is fine, but then you realise that you can't put it where you want to because you already have a piece of scenery there. It is very much like a sudoku puzzle. And that becomes all the more complicated when it is a production which also needs to tour so has to be adaptable for other theatres. You have the idea, and have it all sorted in terms of weight and depth, and then someone says 'but will it work in Plymouth?'

25. LOIS MASKELL

Set designer

One Step Forward, One Step Back a performance by *dreamthinkspeak* Liverpool Anglican Cathedral (April 2008)

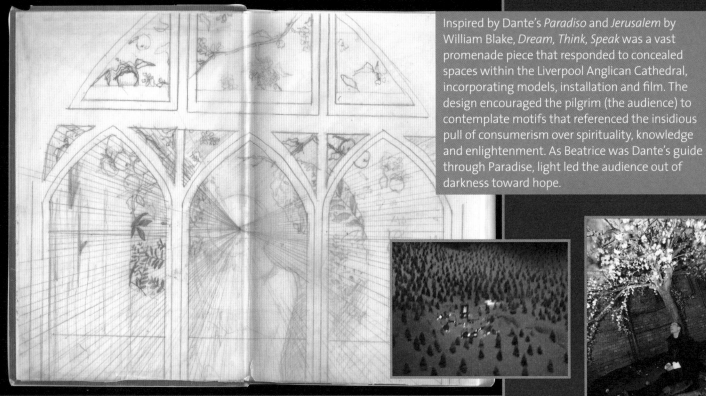

Inspired by Dante's *Paradiso* and *Jerusalem* by William Blake, *Dream, Think, Speak* was a vast promenade piece that responded to concealed spaces within the Liverpool Anglican Cathedral, incorporating models, installation and film. The design encouraged the pilgrim (the audience) to contemplate motifs that referenced the insidious pull of consumerism over spirituality, knowledge and enlightenment. As Beatrice was Dante's guide through Paradise, light led the audience out of darkness toward hope.

Images © Lois Maskell

26. GARY MCCANN

Set and costume designer

Norma, National Opera of Moldova (February 2010)

Images © Gary McCann

Bellini set his opera in ancient Gaul under Roman occupation, which was updated in our production to a futuristic warzone. Costumes were inspired by Science Fiction illustrator Enki Bilal, and combined Roman and Gallic elements with modern couture techniques. The entire design process was conducted digitally: the costume designs were layered and photoshopped collages, and the set designs originated as models generated in Cinema 4D.

27. PETER MUMFORD
Set and lighting designer
E=mc², Birmingham Royal Ballet (September 2009)

When David Bintley first approached me to design this piece, he wanted a design that was defined predominantly by light. As someone who trained originally as a stage designer but has probably become better known for my lighting work, this was terrific: a real opportunity to create a space that was a canvas for light. Matthew Hindson's score is divided into four parts: Energy, Mass, Manhattan Project and the Speed of Light. I created four versions of a space that revealed and used light in different ways, both painterly and using the physical power of intense light, particularly in the final section. In order to do this I worked on a number of physical ways to let light into the space. My design work has, over the years, evolved towards a position where I'm specifically interested in a very direct and deliberate relationship between the space and the way it receives, reflects and is defined by, light, and if I'm asked to design a project, I'm looking to create a space that is considered a canvas for light and performance.

Images © Peter Mumford

28. KIMIE NAKANO
Set and costume designer
Vertical Road, Sadler's Wells, London, and touring (October 2010)

Image © Richard Haughton

Images © Laurent Ziegler

Vertical Road draws inspiration from the Sufi tradition, and the Persian poet and philosopher Rumi. Exploring man's earthly nature, his rituals and the consequences of human actions, *Vertical Road* becomes a meditation on the journey from gravity to grace. Rumi wrote that:

I died from minerality and became vegetable;
And from vegetativeness I died and became animal.
I died from animality and became man.
Then why fear disappearance through death?
Next time I shall die
Bringing forth wings and feathers like angels;
After that, soaring higher than angels –
What you cannot imagine,
I shall be that.

29. CHRISTOPHER ORAM

Set and costume designer

Billy Budd, Glyndebourne (May 2010)

The first thing that struck me when I arrived at Glyndebourne was the intimate relationship between the auditorium and the stage – how its shape, materials and finishes were very evocative of nautical forms. As Billy Budd is pressed into service on board *HMS Indomitable*, we wanted to create the sense of claustrophobia he would have felt being trapped on an eighteenth-century man-of-war. Taking reference for the structure of the set from that of a ship stripped of its cladding, the belly of a whale, and the architecture of Glyndebourne itself, we created a 'rib cage' with decks and galleries following the lines of the auditorium, making the audience implicit in the action on-board the ship. Though the set was semi-abstracted, the space still allowed the officers and crew to work this 'ship' in a relatively naturalistic way, helping to convey the relationships and hierarchies on-board an eighteenth-century frigate.

Images © Alastair Muir

30. JOHN PAWSON
Set designer/Architect

Chroma, Royal Opera House, London (November 2006)

Images © Richard Davies

All architecture concerns itself with the way people will use and move through space, but these dynamic issues are obviously heightened on a dance stage. Part of the specific challenge lay in the way that, unusually for an architect, work of this nature splits how space will be physically experienced from how it will be seen. We wanted to make something that was comfortable for the dancers to use as well as visually comfortable for the audience.

We started with three versions, each exploring a slightly different set of spatial conditions and colour options – black, white and grey. We built models to give a sense of what the finished spaces would be like, and these models became the focus of a series of conversations. It quickly became clear that a particular version of the white void offered the richest creative possibilities, combining an authentic sense of architectural place with a spatially charged canvas for the architecture of the human body.

The finished set is only a slightly revised version of one of those first models. Although the physical structures are all fixed, light can transform the character of the space – manipulating, for example, our perception of the back plane, which can be made to appear to advance or recede. The idea of the controlled opening was part of the design from the beginning, to frame the void and to act as a means of reading the body operating in space. The significance of the precise dimensions of the aperture had key functional – as well as aesthetic – implications: the slightest manipulation of the frame had an impact on the sightlines from a range of locations within the body of the opera house. The height of the lower edge was of particular concern; too low and you lose the sense of spatial intensity, too high and you lose the dancers' feet.

In the end, the task was to create the best possible container for movement and light – an environment where the eye is free to register the subtlest shifts in the musculature of the body, or in the colour and character of the light. The result is, in one sense, a charged limbo. The irony that the architecture required to create this manifestation of void was actually quite substantial was not lost on the people responsible for its construction, one of whom commented that the set for a 20-minute ballet is an edifice on the scale of a full-scale production of *Carmen*.

31. JOANNA SCOTCHER

Set and costume designer

The Railway Children, Waterloo Station Theatre, London (July 2008)

Images © Simon Annand

Images © James Bullimore

We were inspired by the idea of journeys – not just the emotional journey of the characters, but also the very physical experience of travel that lies at the heart of the Steam Age. The joy of this production was looking at the disused Eurostar station anew. We were breathing life back into this cavernous, empty terminal space, recreating the intimate, steamy world of the Edwardian train station.

32. ASHLEY SHAIRP

Set and costume designer

'Tis Pity She's a Whore, Everyman Playhouse, Liverpool (September 2010)

Images © Sam Heath

One of my key design objectives was to reference the history of the Everyman building (which is now rubble) by highlighting surviving architectural details and creating a space that continued its architectural features. The record of the work consists of essential elements such as research imagery, models in various forms, drawings, sketchbook work, tools and cups of tea (probably the most vital ingredient).

33. RAE SMITH

Set designer

War Horse, Olivier Theatre, National Theatre, London (October 2007)

Images © Simon Annand

Throughout the First World War there was a huge revolutionary movement. As well as the old order of the Empires being changed, and radicalized, there was a huge amount of innovation in technology and manufacturing. The changes were necessary in order to make new weapons quickly enough, and then transport them to the frontlines and trenches fast enough.

As well, there were art movements like the Futurists, who saw the possibility of war as a means to cleanse the dusty dry old orders. In Britain we had the Vorticists, which were basically a direct reaction to the Futurist exhibition in this country – mad, bonkers Marinetti and his declaration that it would be a great thing to cut the apron strings of mother and throw your sons to the blood and mess of war.

I realized that the Vorticists, and the Expressionists, and the paintings of people like Paul Nash, gave you a poetic way of showing the First World War. Indeed their fragmented and fractured environments and the strangely surreal, inhuman landscapes that they painted seemed to represent the individual soldiers' experience of being in the war. I inhabited the character of Nicholls a bit like a method actor would inhabit a character, and I began to draw everything that he would see.

And as I was drawing, and saying should we do it like this, I just ripped up my sketchbook and put it in the theatre model box – suddenly there was a lovely cloud, or a landscape, or a gash.

34. SOUND BOOTH
Curated by Karen Lauke

NELA BROWN
Sound design and composition
Hotel Medea, Arcola Theatre, London

STEVE BROWN
Sound design and composition
The Comedy of Errors, Royal Exchange Theatre, Manchester

GARETH FRY
Sound design
Beauty and the Beast, National Theatre, London

GARETH FRY
Sound design
Sucker Punch, Royal Court Theatre, London

KAREN LAUKE
Sound design and composition
The Odyssey, The Rose Theatre, Lancashire

JOHN LEONARD
Sound design
The Master Builder, The Almeida Theatre, London

TOM LISHMAN
Sound design
Broken Glass, Tricycle Theatre, London

MARK MELVILLE
Sound design and composition
The Snow Queen, The Dukes Theatre, Lancaster

ROGER MILLS
Sound design
At Swim Two Boys, Earthfall Dance Theatre, Cardiff

MIC POOL
Sound and video design
Bad Girls: The Musical, The Garrick Theatre, London

MIC POOL
Sound and video design
Death of a Salesman, West Yorkshire Playhouse, Leeds

BRAD WARD
Sound design
PMQ, Theatre 503, London

LISA WHISTLECROFT
Sound design
The Saturated Moment, Royal Opera House, London

PETE WYER
Sound design
Spooky Action, Miro Dance Theatre, Philadelphia

The *Sound Booth* exhibit offers an opportunity to experience sound design in its various guises. The exhibition showcases the work of sound designers who are involved in all aspects of British theatre. The examples and excerpts on offer range from West End to regional theatre productions.